L . H . M A C E & C O .

L. H. MACE & CO.
1883

Woodenware, Meat Safes, Toys,
Refrigerators, Children's Carriages
and House Furnishing Goods

Illustrated Catalog and Historical Introduction

AMERICAN HISTORICAL CATALOG COLLECTION

THE PYNE PRESS
Princeton

First edition

Library of Congress Catalog Card Number 77–146204

ISBN 0–87861–002–2

Printed in the United States of America

Note to the Reader. Reproduction of copy and line drawings are as faithful to the original as is technically possible. Broken type and lines which are uneven or broken can be spotted; these are original! You will understand that manufacturers of such products as woodenware, tinware, glassware and weathervanes were not dedicated to the fine art of printing or involved in the business of publishing. All American Historical Catalog Collection editions are photographed in facsimile from the best available copy, are printed on an especially receptive offset paper, and are strongly bound.

INDEX.

WOODENWARE.

Where no Discount is stated, the prices are Net.

EXCELSIOR WATER TANK

FOR

REFRIGERATORS.

PATENTED MARCH 29TH, 1881.

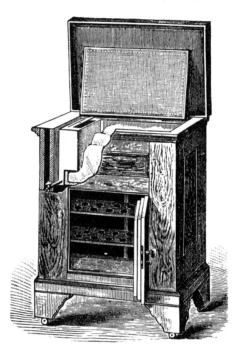

NO.	SUITABLE FOR	CAPACITY ABOUT.	EACH.
1	No. 1 Diamond Upright....	2 Quarts.	**$1.00**
2	No. 1 Excelsior Upright............... .... 2 Diamond "	3 Quarts.	**1.00**
3	No. 2 Excelsior Upright.. .... 3 Diamond "	4 Quarts.	**1.12**
4	No. 3 Excelsior Upright.......... .... 4 Diamond "	5 Quarts.	**1.25**
5	Nos. 4, 5, 6 and 7 Excelsior Upright .. .. 5 and 6 Diamond Upright............	6 Quarts.	**1.50**

A perfectly tight Water Tank alongside or near the ice, which is intended to have pure water placed in it as often as necessary, which will be sufficiently cooled by its close proximity to the ice for all ordinary purposes; if, however, colder water is desired, it can be obtained by putting a small quantity of ice in the Tank. Faucets included in above price.

NURSERY REFRIGERATOR.

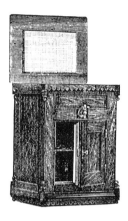

LENGTH.	WIDTH.	HEIGHT.	BLACK WALNUT.
20 inches.	16 inches.	26 inches.	**$12.00**

Fully represented by above cut, made of Black Walnut, finely finished.

THE EXCELSIOR

CORRUGATED GALVANIZED WROUGHT-IRON BOTTOM OR ICE-BACK.

PATENTED MARCH 3D, 1868; MARCH 23D, 1869.

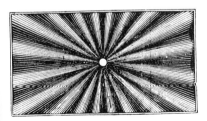

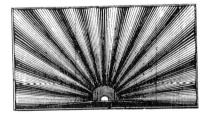

CHEST FORM.   UPRIGHT FORM.

The **Excelsior Bottoms** correspond in size with our make of Excelsior Refrigerators.

They are impenetrable to the ice-pick with ordinary use.

Will not rust. Cannot break. Do away with all Wood Racks.

In ordering the different sizes and kinds for repairing Refrigerators, please state the Number of the Refrigerator, and whether it is the Excelsior Chest or Upright.

DIAMOND
CHEST REFRIGERATOR.

PATENTED.

WHITE

NO.	LENGTH.	WIDTH.	HEIGHT.	IMITATION OAK.
1	25 inches.	18 inches.	24 inches.	$2.75
2	26 "	19½ "	25½ "	3.75
3	29 "	21 "	27 "	5.25
4	32 "	22 "	28 "	6.50
5	35 "	23 "	29 "	7.50
6	38 "	24 "	30 "	8.75
7	44 "	25 "	31 "	10.50
8	50 "	25 "	31 "	12.50

The **Diamond Chest Refrigerator** is made of Pine, painted in imitation of Oak, with dark panels, has an inside box, plain galvanized iron bottom, zinc lining, shelves, casters, suitable fittings, etc.

This **Refrigerator** having proved good selling, cheap and satisfactory, we offer it as our Second Quality, claiming it to be the best that can be produced for the price.

EXCELSIOR
CHEST REFRIGERATOR,

With the Excelsior Wrought-Iron Bottom.

PATENTED.

WHITE

NO.	LENGTH.	WIDTH.	HEIGHT.	IMITATION OAK.
1	25 inches.	18 inches.	24 inches.	$3.25
2	26 "	19½ "	25½ "	4 50
3	29 "	21 "	27 "	6.50
4	32 "	22 "	28 "	8.00
5	35 "	23 "	29 "	9.50
6	38 "	24 "	30 "	11.00
7	44 "	25 "	31 "	13.00
8	50 "	25 "	31 "	15.00

The **Excelsior Chest Refrigerator** is made of well-seasoned Pine, painted in imitation of Oak, with a perfectly tight inside box, of Spruce, leaving a closed air space as a non conductor. Zinc Lining, Shelves, Casters, suitable Fittings, etc. Constructed in the best manner of the best material.

This **Refrigerator** has the Ice placed in the bottom, and it therefore consumes less ice than the Upright, from the well-known principle that warm air rises and cold air falls. We strongly recommend it where ice is very expensive, as in all tropical regions.

DIAMOND
UPRIGHT REFRIGERATOR.

PATENTED.

NO.	LENGTH.	WIDTH.	HEIGHT.	IMITATION OAK.
1	23 inches.	17 inches.	37 inches.	**$6.00**
2	26 "	18 "	39 "	**7.00**
3	29 "	19 "	41 "	**8.50**
4	32 "	21 "	43 "	**10.00**
5	35 "	23 "	45 "	**12.00**
6	38 "	23 "	47 "	**15.00**

Double—two doors and two separate apartments.

The **Diamond Upright Refrigerator** is made of Pine, painted in imitation of Oak, with dark panels; has an inside box, plain galvanized iron bottom, zinc lining and shelves, casters, suitable fittings, etc.

This **Refrigerator** we offer as our second quality; for cheapness, strength and durability it cannot be surpassed.

NOTICE difference in measurements of similar numbers of the Diamond and Excelsior Uprights.

EXCELSIOR
Upright Improved Refrigerator,

With the Excelsior Wrought-Iron Bottom.

PATENTED.

NO.	LENGTH.	WIDTH.	HEIGHT.	IMITATION OAK.
1	26 inches.	18 inches.	39 inches.	**$9.00**
2	29 "	19 "	41 "	**11.00**
3	32 "	21 "	43 "	**13.00**
4	35 "	23 "	45 "	**15.00**

The **Excelsior Upright Refrigerator** we claim to be the best family Refrigerator in the market. The door of this Refrigerator, opening below the ice, causes a slight change of air, and makes it self-ventilating. Our many improvements make this a cold dry-air Refrigerator, and its contents are always free from dampness and all impurities or odors, rendering it capable of preserving articles much longer and in better condition than any other form of Refrigerator.

Constructed similar to the Excelsior Chest (page 5), in the best manner and of the best material.

EXCELSIOR DOUBLE

Upright Improved Refrigerator,

With the Excelsior Wrought-Iron Bottom.

PATENTED.

NO.	LENGTH.	WIDTH.	HEIGHT.	IMITATION OAK.
5	38 inches.	23 inches.	47 inches.	**$20.00**
6	44 "	23 "	49 "	**24.00**
7	50 "	24 "	49 "	**30.00**
	Wine Cooler in the top.			

The **Excelsior Double Upright Refrigerator** is constructed on the same principle as the Excelsior Upright (page 7), the provision chamber is divided into separate apartments by a zinc partition, perforated to admit the free passage of air from one side to the other, and separate doors, both of which lock with a substantial mortise lock.

Constructed similar to the Excelsior Chest (page 5), in the best manner and of the best material.

EXTRA

Excelsior Chest Refrigerator,

With the Excelsior Wrought-Iron Bottom.

PATENTED.

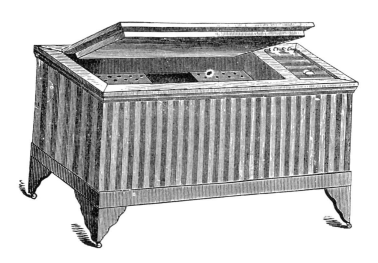

NO.	LENGTH.	WIDTH.	HEIGHT.	ASH.
8½	44 inches.	24 inches.	30 inches.	$20.00
9	50 "	25 "	33 "	24.00
10	56 "	28 "	35 "	28.00
11	62 "	31 "	37 "	32 00

The **Extra Excelsior Chest Refrigerator** is made of Ash, with nickel-plated trimmings, and finished extra strong. Has an inside box covered with felt paper, leaving a closed air space as a non-conductor; inside lining and shelves of zinc. The small chamber is for ice, and the large chamber shelved for provisions. We recommend them to give perfect satisfaction.

EXTRA EXCELSIOR

Upright Improved Refrigerator.

PATENTED.

NO.	LENGTH.	WIDTH.	HEIGHT.	ASH.
A	32 inches.	22 inches.	49 inches.	**$20.00**
B	35 "	24 "	52 "	**24.00**

The **Extra Excelsior Upright Improved Refrigerator** is constructed on the same principle as the Excelsior Upright (page 7). They are made of Ash, with nickel-plated trimmings, and finished extra strong. Has an inside box covered with felt paper, leaving a closed air space as a non-conductor; inside lining and shelves of zinc. We recommend them to give perfect satisfaction.

EXTRA EXCELSIOR

Upright Improved Refrigerator.

PATENTED.

NO.	LENGTH.	WIDTH.	HEIGHT.	ASH.
8	39 inches.	24 inches.	57 inches.	**$32.00**
9	45 "	26 "	59 "	**40.00**
10	51 "	28 "	61 "	**48.00**
11	57 "	30 "	63 "	**56.00**

The **Extra Excelsior Upright Improved Refrigerator** is constructed on the same principle as described on page 7.

In these Refrigerators there is no wood exposed to the ice or provisions; every part is lined either with zinc or galvanized iron. Finished extra strong, in the best manner and of the best material, as per page 10.

GROCER'S REFRIGERATOR,

With Sliding Covers and Galvanized Iron Bottom.

PATENTED.

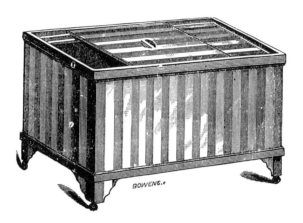

NO.	LENGTH.	WIDTH.	HEIGHT.	GRANITE.	ASH.
2	44 inches.	25 inches.	31 inches.	**$12.00**	**$15.00**
3	50 "	27 "	33 "	**14.00**	**18.00**
4	56 "	29 "	35 "	**16.00**	**21.00**
5	62 "	31 "	37 "	**18.00**	**24.00**
6	74 "	31 "	37 "		**30.00**

Larger sizes made to order.

The above cut represents a **Sliding Cover Grocer's Refrigerator,** for the use of Butchers, Grocers, Saloons, or other purposes where a large and extra strong Refrigerator is required.

They are made of Ash, have an inside box covered with felt paper, leaving a closed air space between the two; inside lining of zinc.

The covers slide on ways, one above the other, making it more convenient to place under a counter or shelf than it would be if they raised.

There are no shelves, cleats, or other fixtures inside, but may be furnished to order.

Nos. 2, 3, 4 and 5 are also made of Pine, and painted in imitation of Granite.

REFRIGERATOR

FOR BUTTER, FISH OR FRUIT DEALERS,

DINING SALOONS, HOTELS, ETC.

PATENTED.

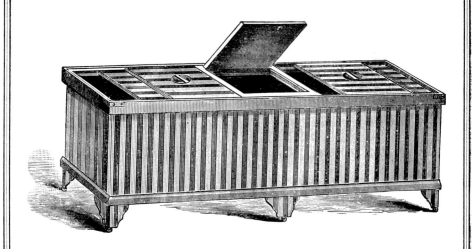

LENGTH.	WIDTH.	HEIGHT.	ASH.
9 foot.	26 inches.	37 inches.	**$40.00**

ANY SIZE DESIRED MADE TO ORDER.

The above cut represents a Refrigerator for the use of **Butter, Fish or Fruit Dealers,** or other purposes where a large and extra strong Refrigerator is required.

They are made of ash; have an inside box covered with felt paper, leaving a closed air space between the two; inside lining and shelves of zinc. Ice box in the centre of Refrigerator, with openings for the circulation of air. Sliding covers over each provision apartment.

LAGER BEER REFRIGERATOR,

Made of Ash.

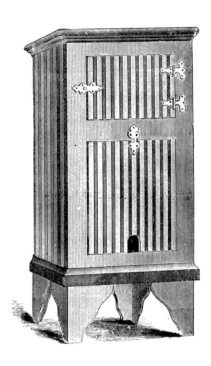

NO.	LENGTH.	WIDTH.	HEIGHT.	ASH.
1	28 inches.	31 inches.	60 inches.	**$18.00**

    The above cut represents the **Single Upright Lager Beer Refrigerator**, used for the purpose of keeping beer cool while on draught; the ice chamber is on the top, with openings for the circulation of air, is made very strong, and is large enough to contain ice, cold cuts, bottles, and other articles that it is desired to keep cool.

    They are made of ash, with nickel-plated trimmings.

LAGER BEER REFRIGERATOR,

Made of Ash.

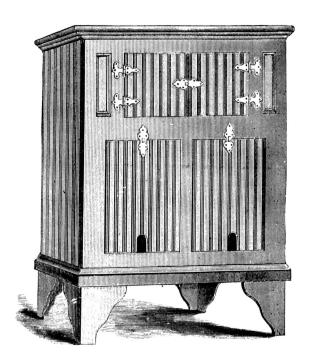

NO.	LENGTH.	WIDTH.	HEIGHT.	ASH.
2	48 inches.	31 inches.	60 inches.	**$31.50**

The above cut represents the **Double Lager Beer Upright Refrigerator.** It does not differ from No. 1 in construction, except being large enough to contain two kegs instead of one, which is a great saving where a keg is wanted every hour or two —one keg cooling while the other is being drawn from—thus being always cool.

COMBINATION
LAGER BEER REFRIGERATOR,

Made of Ash.

NO.	LENGTH.	WIDTH.	HEIGHT.	ASH.
4	48 inches.	31 inches.	76 inches.	**$45.00**

The above cut represents the **Combination Lager Beer Refrigerator,** made of Ash, with nickel-plated trimmings, handsomely finished. The lower part is a provision chamber, which can also be used for cooling two kegs of beer, simply by removing the shelves, thus holding four kegs.

COMBINATION

LAGER BEER REFRIGERATOR,

Made of Ash.

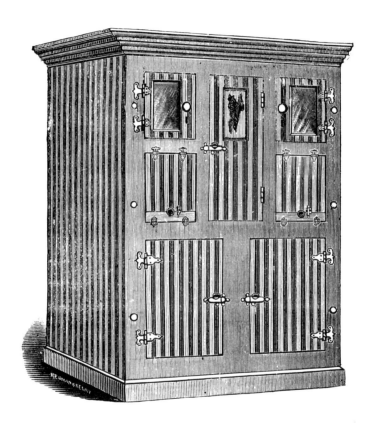

NO.	LENGTH.	WIDTH.	HEIGHT.	ASH.
5	78 inches.	36 inches.	84 inches.	**$100.00**

The above cut represents **Lager Beer Refrigerator No. 5,** made of Ash, with nickel-plated Trimmings, handsomely finished, and capable of holding eight kegs of beer; can be taken apart.

SINGLE MEAT SAFES.

KNOCK DOWN FOR SHIPPING.

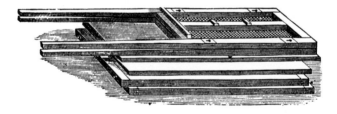

The **Meat Safe** packed ready for boxing. It now occupies about one-quarter the room.

NO.	LENGTH.	WIDTH.	HEIGHT.	IMITATION OAK.
1	30 inches.	16 inches.	46 inches.	**$4.00**
2	34 "	17 "	48 "	**4.75**
3	38 "	18 "	50 "	**5 50**
4	42 "	19 "	52 "	**6.00**
5	46 "	20 "	54 "	**6.75**

The **Meat Safe** can be taken entirely apart by removing six screws from the top. It is made of Pine, with fine mesh Wire Cloth, finished in the best manner, and painted in imitation of Oak. *Specially adapted for Export Trade.*

DOUBLE MEAT SAFES,

TWO APARTMENTS.

KNOCK DOWN.

PATENTED JANUARY 29TH, 1867.

NO.	LENGTH.	WIDTH.	HEIGHT.	IMITATION OAK.
1	30 inches.	16 inches.	52 inches.	**$7.50**
2	34 "	17 "	54 "	**8.75**
3	38 "	18 "	56 "	**9.75**
4	42 "	19 "	58 "	**11.00**
5	46 "	20 "	60 "	**12.00**

The **Meat Safe** can be taken entirely apart by removing six screws from the top. It is made of Pine, with fine mesh Wire Cloth, finished in the best manner, and painted in imitation of Oak. *Specially adapted for Export Trade.*

WATER COOLERS.

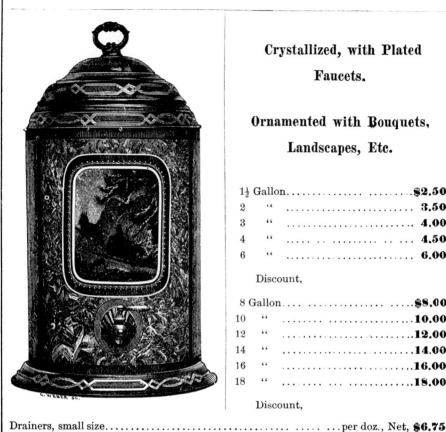

Crystallized, with Plated Faucets.

Ornamented with Bouquets, Landscapes, Etc.

1½ Gallon......................	**$2.50**
2 "	**3.50**
3 "	**4.00**
4 "	**4.50**
6 "	**6.00**

Discount,

8 Gallon....	**$8.00**
10 "	**10.00**
12 "	**12.00**
14 "	**14.00**
16 "	**16.00**
18 "	**18.00**

Discount,

Drainers, small size..................................... ....per doz., Net,		**$6.75**
" large " .... "	"	**8.10**
Water Cooler Stands, small size.................................Each,	"	**3.25**
" " large " .... "	"	**4.00**

Water Coolers.

MADE OF ASH.

12 Gallon..............Each, Net,			**$10.00**
16 " .. .. "	"		**13.00**
28 " .... "	"		**16.00**

ICE CREAM FREEZERS.

Double Action Top Crank Freezer.

Good, reliable and cheap.

2 Quart		$2.50
3 "		3.00
4 "		4.00
6 "		5.00
8 "		6.00
10 "		7.50

Discount.

Double Action Side Crank Freezers.

Good, reliable and cheap.

2 Quart		$3.00
3 "		3.50
4 "		4.50
6 "		5.50
8 "		6.50
10 "		8.00

Discount.

Celebrated Triple Motion White Mountain Freezers.

SAND'S PATENT.

2 Quart		$3.75
3 "		4.50
4 "		5.50
6 "		7.00
8 "		8.00
10 "		10.00
15 "		15.00
20 "		20.00
25 "		25.00

Discount.

Net.

Fly Wheels for Freezers $3.75
Ice Crusher, small............. 5.50

Catalogues of Platform and Power Freezers furnished on application.

VALENTINE'S PATENT FELT WEATHER STRIP.

PATENTED JANUARY 12TH, 1875.

This Strip is made of neatly molded Black Walnut, well smoothed and finished in oil. The **Felt** is of the best California Wool, and prepared by a process which renders it both **Water-Proof** and **Moth-Proof.**

We recommend it as the latest and best kind of Weather Strip in the market. Send for samples and circulars, with full description and prices.

No. 0.

No. 1.

No. 0...................................	**4c.** per foot.	⎫
" 1....................................	**5c.** " "	
" 2....................................	**9c.** " "	
" 3....................................	**9c.** " "	⎬ Discount.
" 4....................................	**7c.** " "	
" 5....................................	**12c.** " "	⎭

Cotton's Folding Settee.

View when Opened.   *View when Closed.*

This is the most convenient Settee for camp-meetings, excursions, picnics, lawns, and play-grounds ever offered to the trade. It can be closely folded and easily carried from place to place in the hand, and, when adjusted for use, will accommodate three persons of ordinary size. We manufacture these Settees four feet in length, with easy back and slat spring seat. They are nicely finished in two coats of red and varnished.

Price, per dozen **$13.00**

American Fancy Lap Boards,

Made of different kinds and colors of wood, put together with patent dovetail joints, in representation of inlaid work.

Price, per doz. $9.00

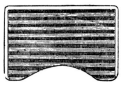

Lap Boards.

Per doz.

Plain White Wood $6.00
"   "   "   with feet... ... 7.00

Indispensable for ladies' use in cutting, basting, etc.

VIEW WHEN OPEN

VIEW WHEN CLOSED.

Folding Lap Boards.

COTTON'S PATENT.

Constructed of alternate strips of Black Walnut and Pine, securely fastened to cloth, thus making them flexible and folding; finished nicely, and have stamped upon them a yard measure; convenient, strong, and will not warp.

Price, per doz..... ...   .$9.00

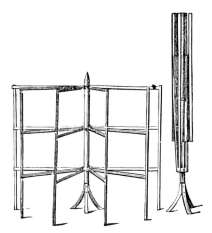

Clothes Dryers.

BOOTH'S PATENT.

Per doz.

4 Arm Dryer......................$9.00
6 "   " 12.00

Made very light, yet substantial, with circular Bolts running through the Bars, with Thumb Nuts to regulate them, so that they may be made to stand at any angle, well braced, etc.

Wood Table Mats.

SIX IN A SET.

Made of alternate strips of light and dark wood, polished, fastened securely to cloth, thus making them flexible, and finished in a fine manner. Put up six in a set, containing

   2 Mats, 6 in. wide by 8 in. long.
   2 "   8   "   10   "
   2 "   9   "   12   "

Light shade, per dozen sets........**$6.00**
Dark   "   " **6.50**

Butler's Trays.

	Per doz.
No. 1, Ash, 17x29..................	**$18.00**
" 2, " 19x31.	**20.25**
" 3, " 21x33..............	**22.50**
Stands, "	**11.25**
No. 1, Black Walnut, 17x29......	**20.25**
" 2, " " 19x31.......	**22.50**
" 3, " " 21x33......	**24.75**
Stands, " "	**11.25**

Knife Trays.

	Per doz.
No. A, Striped Straight Sides, as per above cut................	**$6.75**
" 4, Flare Sides, Striped, as per above cut................	**9.00**
" 1, Three Apartments, Straight Sides, Striped, as per above cut....	**11.25**

Knife Trays.

	Per doz.
No. 10, Small, Flare Sides, White Wood.......	**$1.00**
" 11, Small, Flare Sides, White Wood..........	**1.50**
" 6, Small, Flare Sides, White Wood	**2.25**
" 9, Large, Flare Sides, White Wood...................	**3.00**
" 5, Small, Flare Sides, Black Walnut....	**5.63**
" 8, Large, Flare Sides, Black Walnut................	**6.75**

Kitchen Tables.

		Per doz.
3 feet, Pine, Plain	....	$15.75
4 " "	....	22.50
5 " "	....	29.25
6 " "	....	36.00

With Drawers, **75c.** Extra, Each.

Settee Tables.

	Per doz.
4 feet, Pine....................	$40.50
5 "	.... 54.00
6 "	.... 63.00

With Apartments for Irons, Blankets. etc.

Skirt Boards.

		Per doz.
3 feet Pine.	......	$3.60
3½ "	....	4.50
4 "	....	5.40
4½ "	....	6.30
5 "	....	7.20
5½ "	....	8.10
6 "	....	9.00

With Feet, **35c.** Extra, Each.

Sleeve Boards.

	Per doz.
Pine..........................	$1.50
Black Walnut	3.00

Clothes Horses.

		Per doz.
3 feet Pine....	....	$5.40
4 " "	....	9.00
5 " "	....	11.25
6 " "	....	13.50
6 " 4 Bar	....	14.85
7 " 4 "	....	18.00

Round Bar (Nursery).

		Per doz.
3 Fect, 2 Fold	....	$2.60
3 " 3 "	....	3.75
3 " 4 "	....	5.25
3 " 5 "	....	6.50
3½ " 3 "	....	3.60
4 "	....	5.00
5 "	....	7.00
6 "	....	12.00

Foot Benches.

Per doz.

Pine	$2.00
Hardwood, Painted	2.50
Black Walnut, Plain	6.00
" Carpeted	9.00

Pantry Steps.

Per doz.

Pine, 2 feet	$7.20
" 3 "	9.00
Black Walnut, 2 feet	15.75
" 3 "	20.25

Library Cricket Steps.

Per doz.

Ash	$13.50
Black Walnut	15.75
" Carpeted	20.25

Library Folding Steps.

Per doz.

Ash	$22.50
Black Walnut	27.00
" Carpeted	33.75
" " extra	38.25

V Folding Ladders.

Per doz.

2 feet, Pine			**$8.10**
3 " "			**11.25**
4 " "			**15.75**
2 " Black Walnut			**13.50**
3 " "			**18.00**
4 " "			**27.00**

Shelf Ladders.

Per doz.

4 feet, Pine		**$9.00**
5 "		**11.25**
6 "		**13.50**
7 "		**15.75**
8 "		**18.00**
9 "		**22.50**

Step Ladders.

Per doz.

4 feet, Pine		**$13.50**
5 "		**15.75**
6 "		**18.00**
7 "		**22.50**
8 "		**27.00**
9 "		**31.50**

Udell's Patent Ladders.

Excelsior.

Each.

3 feet		**$2.50**
4 "		**3.00**
5 "		**3.50**
6 "		**4.00**
7 "		**4.50**
8 "		**5.00**
9 "		**5.50**
10 "		**6.00**
12 "		**8.00**

Discount, 50 and 10 per cent.

Pails.

	Per doz.
Oak Grained, Half Pails	**$1.30**
"　　2 Hoops..............	**1.60**
"　　3　"	**1.75**
"　　2　"　Best........	**1.70**
"　　3　"	**1.90**
"　　3　"　Riveted Ear..	**2.25**
Assorted Colors, 2 Hoops....... ..	**1.75**
"　　　　3　"	**2.00**
Pine, Brass Bound, 2 Hoops........	**2.75**
"　　"　　"　3　"	**3.00**
Cedar, Galvanized, 3　"	**4.25**
"　Brass Bound, 3　"　Small ..	**4.25**
"　　"　　"　3　"　Med....	**4.75**
"　　"　　"　3　"　Large ..	**5.25**
"　B.B., Striped, 3　"　Med ..	**6.50**
"　　"　　"　3　"　Large ..	**7.50**
White Pine, Stable, Flush Bottom.	**2.50**
Oak Grained　　"　　"	**3.00**
Ash, Stable, Small,　"　　"	**5.25**
"　　"　Large,　"　　"	**6.00**
Oak,　"　Small,　"　　"	**6.50**
"　　"　Large,　"　　"	**7.50**
"　　"　　"　　"　　"	**8.50**

Tubs.

	Per Nest.
Pine, Blue or Oak Grained—	
8 in Nest.....................	**$2.35**
3　"	**1.60**
Cedar, Best—	
3 in Nest, Plain Iron...........	
3　"　Galvanized Iron.....	

Brooms.

	Per doz.
No. 6, Shaker.....................	**$2.25**
"　7,　"	**2.50**
"　8,　"	**2.75**
"　6, Velvet Shaker	**2.50**
"　7,　"	**2.75**
"　8,　"	**3.00**
"　6, Plain Hurl	**2.50**
"　7,　"	**2.75**
"　8,　"	**3.00**
"　6, Fancy Handle Hurl.........	**3.00**
"　7,　"　"	**3.25**
"　8,　"　"	**3.50**
"　9,　"　"	**4.00**
"　6, Velvet Hurl, Ex. Green Corn	**3.25**
"　7,　"　"　"	**3.50**
"　8,　"　"　"	**3.75**
"　9,　"　"　"	**4.25**
1, String, Hearth or Toy Brooms ..	**0.85**
2,　"　"　"　"	**...1.00**
14-inch. Street or Stable Brooms	**...4.60**
16　"　"　"　"	**.....5.25**
Flat Rattan, Stable Brooms....	**5.00**

Wash Boards.

	Per doz.
Wood...........................	**$1.20**
Zinc, Single.	**1.50**
"　Raised Centers	**1.75**
"　Double	**2.00**
"　"　New Crimp	**2.15**
"　Single Protector........	**2.65**
"　Double　"	**3.00**
"　"　Wilson's Patent	**2.75**
"　"　Medium.............	**2.75**
"　"　Medium, New Crimp..	**2.75**
"　and Wood Combination.. ...	**2.75**
"　Single Laundry..........	**3.25**
"　Double　"	**4.25**
"　"　"　New Crimp..	**4.50**

Keelers.

Per Nest.

Pine, Painted, 5 in Nest..........	$0.85
Cedar, Round, Gal. Hoop, 4 in Nest	1.65
Cedar, Round, B. B., Plain, 4 in Nest...................	2.00
Cedar, Oval, B. B., Plain, 5 in Nest	6.50
Cedar, Round, B. B., Striped, 4 in Nest....................	2.50
Cedar, Oval, B. B., Striped, 5 in Nest	7.00

Per doz.

Cedar, Small, for Refrigerators....	$4.80
" Large, " "	6.50

Baskets.

Per doz:

Willow, School........	$2.00 to $3.00

Per Nest.

Willow, Market, 4 in Nest,	$1.50 to $2.75

Per doz.

Ex. Splint, Cov. Mkt., No. 1.......	$3.00
" " " " " 2.......	3.75
" " " " " 3......	4.25
" " " " " 4.......	5.50
Cedar Wood, Cov. Mkt., 9 in......	3.75
" " " " 10 "....	4.25
" " " " 12 ".....	5.25
" " " " 14 "....	6.50
" " " " 16 "...	7.50
" " " " 18 ".....	9.00
Willow, Braid, Ex. fine, Cov., No. 1..	9.85
" " " " " 2..	11.75
" " " " " 3..	13.50
" " " " " 4..	15.00

Clothes.

Willow, Oval, Small............ ...	$6.50
" " Medium............	7.50
" " Large.	9.00
Rattan, Laundry, No. 1...........	6.25
" " " 2....	7.25
" " " 3...........	8.00
" " " 4...........	9.00

Per Nest.

Rattan, Oblong, 4 in Nest..	$2.50
" Oval, Pat. Bot., 4 in Nest..	3.00
Willow, " Com., 4 in Nest......	2.50
" " Ex., 4 "	3.75
" " Ex. Heavy, 5 in Nest.	6.50
" Square, " 5 "	7.00
" Hampers, Square, 3 "	7.00

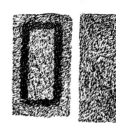

Door Mats.

Per doz.

No. 1, Common Coir...........	$5.00
" 2, " "	7.00
" 3, " "	9.00
" 1, Solid "	7.50
" 2, " "	9.50
" 3, " "	11.00
" 1, " " Extra........	10.50
" 2, " " "	13.00
" 3. " " "	16.50
" 1, " " Oval..........	9.00
" 2, " " "	11.00
" 3, " " ..."	13.50

Cordage.

Rope, Jute.....	
" Sisal.......................	
" Manilla...................	

Per doz.

Jute Pulley Lines, 50 feet.........	$1.10
" " " 72 "	1.40
" " " 100 "	2.00
" Clothes " hand - made, 75 feet..........	2.25
Jute Clothes Lines, hand-made, 100 feet.........................	3.25

Twines.

Per lb.

Cotton..........	.23 to 30c.
Hemp.......................	.22 to 25c.
Flax	.23 to 30c.
Wicking	.22 to 30c.
Sash Cord, common.................	20c.
" patent....	21c.

Churns.

Oak.	Each.
No. 1, 7 gallons..............	$1.60
2, 8 "	1.80
3, 9 "	2.00
4, 10 "	2.25
5, 11 "	2.50
6, 12 "	2.75
7, 13½ "	3.00
8, 14½ "	3.25
9, 16 "	3.50

Discount, 20 per cent.

Flour Pails.

	Per doz.
Small............................	$2.25
Medium...........	3.00
Large	5.00
Nested 3 in....	9.50
Best, Small.......................	2.50
" Medium.................	3.75
" Large.	5.50
" Nested 3 in	11.00

Sieves.

	Per doz.
Flour, Nested 3 in Plated Wire.....	$1.25
Coal Sifters, Nested 3 in....	1.15
" " " 2 in...........	1.25
Rival Ash Sifters..................	7.00

Nest Boxes.

	Per doz.
Plain, Nested 5 in...................	$3.50
Varnished, Nested 5 in............	4.50
Saratoga Spice, 4 in................	4.00
Tin Rimmed Spice.....	8.50
Wood, Black Walnut, Spice.	8.50
Tin Rimmed, Nested 5 in..........	9.50

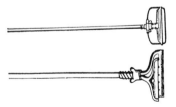

Mop Handles.

	Per doz.
Iron, Patent......	$1.50
Mop and Brush Holders..	1.70

Universal Wringers.

	Per doz.
No. 2½, Usual Family Size.......	$40.00
" 2, Medium " "	43.00
" 1½, Large " "	50.50
" 1, " Laundry Size........	64.00

Butter

Prints.		Moulds.	
	Per doz.		Per doz.
2 in	$0.90	1-32 lb	$1.80
2½ "	1.00	1-16 "	2.00
3 "	1.15		
3¼ "	1.20	1-8 "	2.65
3½ "	1.30		
3¾ "	1.50	1-4 "	3.90
4 "	1.65	1-2 "	5.00
4¼ "	1.90		
4½ "	2.25	1 "	6.25

Butter Spades.

Plain..... **$0.65**   Grooved...... **$0.75**

Measures.

	Per doz.
Wood, Plain, Nested 5 in	$6.50
1 Quart, Wood, Plain	0.90
2 " " "	1.25
4 " " "	1.50
8 " " "	2.00
16 " " "	2.50
2 " Iron Bound	1.75
4 " "	2.00
8 " "	2.60
16 " "	3.50
Iron Bound, Nest 5 in	9.50

Barrel Covers.

	Per doz.
½ Barrel Covers.	$1.10
19 inches diameter	1.35
21 " "	1.75
19 " " Chestnut	2.75
21 " " "	3.00

Bowls.

	Per doz.
No. 1, Round, 11 in	$1.00
" 2, " 13 "	1.50
" 3, " 15 "	2.10
" 4, " 17 "	3.25
" 5, " 19 "	4.25
" 6, " 21 "	5.50
" 7, " 24 "	8.00

Trays.

	Per doz.
No. 1, Oval, 17 inch	$2.00
" 2, " 20 "	2.75
" 3, " 23 "	4.00
" 4, " 25 "	5.00

Salt Boxes.

	Per doz.
Small	$2.00
Large	$3.00

Butter Ladles.

Per doz.

Common $0.75
Half-Size $0.90
Good........... .... 1.00
Extra.... .... 1.15

Lemon Squeezers.

Per doz.

Wood, Small, Best.... ....$1.00
" Large...................... 1.25
Sammis, Pat., Galvanized Iron. ... 3.75

Steak Mauls.

Per doz.

Small................. .. ..$0.90
Large 1.00

Potato Mashers.

Per doz.

Small....... ....$0.65
Large 0.90

Spoons.

Per doz.

Soft Wood.... ....$0.30
Turned.......................... 0.60
Day's 0.75
Soft Wood, Large........... ...... 0.90
Salad Forks and Spoons, Boxwood, 2.00 to 2.50
Mustard, Boxwood, per gross 2.25

Long Handle Ladles.

Per doz.

Small......... ....$0.90
Large... .... 1.00

Whisk Brushes.

Per doz.

	Per doz.
Wood Handle, Plain	$0.90
" " Enameled	1.00
Hurl Handle, Pocket	1.10
Enameled " "	1.50
No. 1, Hurl Handle	1.50
" 2, " "	1.75
" 3, " "	2.00
" 1, " " Best	1.75
" 2, " " "	2.00
" 3, " " "	2.25
" 1, Enamel Wood Handle	1.85
" 2, " " "	2.00
" 1, White " "	2.25
" 2, " " "	2.50

Bone Handle Whisks in variety.

Toy Brushes.

Per doz.

5 inch Block, White Tampico......$0.35

Nail Brushes.

Per doz.

4½ inch Block, White Tampico.....$0.50

Stove Brushes.

Per doz.

			Per doz.
No. 0, Black Tampico, 9½ in.			$1.00
" 1, " " 9¼ in.			1.35
" 4, Gray " 10 in.			1.75
" 10, " Bristles			2.25
" Tampico, Curved Back.			2.00

Sink Brushes.

Per doz.

	Per doz.
Corn	$0.40
Heather	.50
Coir, White Handle	.75
" Black "	.85

Scrubbing Brushes.

Per doz.

				Per doz.
No. 1, White Tampico, 8 in. Block.				$0.55
" 100, " " 7 in. "				.55
" 102, " " 8 in. "				.75
" 102, Gray " 8 in. "				.80
" 104, White " 9 in. "				.85
" 104, Gray " 9 in. "				.90
" 106, White " 10 in. "				.95
" 106, Gray " 10 in. "				1.10
" 104, " Bristles, 9 in. "				1.75
" 106, " " 10 in. "				2.00

Sea Root Scrubs.

Per doz.

	Per doz.
No. 1	$0.90
" 2	1.00
" 3	1.10
" 4	1.25

Shoe Brushes.

No.				Per doz.
11, Tampico Top Knot, no handle				$0.90
12, " " "				1.10
1, Oval Tampico, as per cut				1.00
2, " " "				1.35
4, " " "				1.75
31, " Bristles, "				1.50
32, " " "				1.85
44, " " "				2.00
33, " " large, as per cut				2.25
22, " " as per cut				2.25
45, " " large, as per cut				2.75
60, " " "				3.25
62, " " polishing, "				2.25
Porter's Horse-hair, small				4.00
" " large				5.00
No. 2, Dauber's Tampico				.75
" 3, " Bristles				.90
" 5, " Horse-hair				1.25

Wing Scrub Brushes.

Per doz.

			Per doz.
No. 28, White Tampico, 10 in.			$1.25
" 28, Gray " 10 in.			1.35
" 30, White " 11 in.			1.35
" 30, Gray " 11 in.			1.50
" 50, " Bristle.			2.50

Steamboat Scrubs.

HOLLOWED SIDES.

Per doz.

			Per doz.
No. 1, White Tampico			$1.30
" 2, " "			1.40
" 3, " "			1.50
" 1, " Centre, Gray Ends			1.35
" 1, Gray Bristles			2.50
" 2, " "			2.75

Cocoa Dippers.

Per doz.
Tin Rimmed **$2.25**

Rolling Pins.

Per doz.
Stationary Handle **$0.75**
Revolving   " **1.00**

Dusters.

Turkey Feathers.		Counter Dusters.	
	Per doz.		Per doz.
No. 10	**$12.60**	No. 1	**$2.00**
" 11	**15.00**	" 2.	**2.50**
" 12..	**18.00**	" 3	**3.00**
" 13	**21.00**	" 5, Extra	**4.50**
" 14	**23.40**	" 6, "	**5.00**
" 15...	**25.20**	" 7, "	**6.50**
" 16	**28.50**	" 8, "	**7.25**

Discount,

School Slates.

	Per doz.
4 x 6 inches ...	**$0.24**
5 x 7 "	**.28**
6 x 9 "	**.38**
6½x10 "	**.40**
7 x11 "	**.45**
8 x12 "	**.60**
9 x13 "	**.70**

Slate Pencils.

Pointed, 100 in Box, per Box..... **$0.20**

Hair Floor Brooms.

Per doz.
No. 11, Small	**$7.25**
" 13, Medium	**9.75**
" 15, Large	**12.25**
" 19, Small, Extra	**16.00**
" 21, Large, "	**19.00**
" 25, Very Best	**22.75**
Pope's Eyes, No. 1	**5.50**
" Heads, No. 0	**6.50**
Window Brushes, Short Handle	**6.00**
" " Long "	**10.50**
6-foot Poles	**1.25**
8-foot "	**1.75**
10-foot "	**2.25**
12-foot "	**2.75**

School Bags.

CLOSE WORK HEMP.

Per doz.
No. 2, 10 x12	**$1.00**
" 3, 11½x14½	**1.20**
" 4, 12 x16	**1.40**

Knife Boards.

Per doz.

No. 1, Short.................... ...$2.70
" 2, " 3.15
" 1, Long 2.25
" 2, " 2.70

Bosom Boards.

Per doz.

Round........................... $1.70
Square........................... 1.70

Meat Boards.

Ash. Per doz.

No. 1, 12 inch by 14 inch..........$2.70
" 2, 14 " 16 " 3.60
" 3, 16 " 18 " 4.50

Boxed.

No. 1, 12 inch by 14 inch.......... 4.50
" 2, 14 " 16 " 5.40
" 3, 16 " 18 " 6.30

Pastry Boards.

Per doz.

No. 0, 14 inch by 20 inch..........$2.70
" 1, 16 " 22 " 3.15
" 2, 18 " 24 " 3.60
" 3, 20 " 27 " 4.05
" 4, 22 " 30 " 4.50

Wash Benches.

Per doz.

3 feet... ....$8.10
4 " 10.35
5 " 12.60
6 " 15.75

Snow Shovels.

Per doz.

Wood, Large.....................$4.00
Patent, Iron-bound " Challenge ".. 4.00
" " " Railroad ".... 4.50
" " " D Handle ". . 5.00

Towel Arms.

Per doz.

No. 2, Plain Black Walnut........$1.50

" 3, " " " silver tips. 2.00

Towel Arms.

Per doz.

No. 4, Black Walnut Arms, silver tips, malleable iron... ...$3.25

Coat Racks.

Per doz.

No. 4, or 4 Hooks.................$1.50

" 5, or 5 " 1.75

" 6, or 6 " 2.00

Extension Racks.

Per doz,

7 Pins, Black Walnut..... ......$1.75

10 " " 2.00

13 " " 2.25

Towel Rollers.

Per doz.

White Wood, Narrow, 18 in........$1.00

"   Wide,   18 " 1.25

Black Walnut Oiled, Open, 18 in... 2.50

"   " Closed, 18 " ... 2.50

"   Van'd, Open, 18 " ... 3.00

"   " Closed, 18 " ... 3.00

Spruce, Ex. Large,   "   20 " ... 3.00

Blk. Wal.,   "   "   20 " ... 3.50

Fly Traps.

Per doz.

Balloon ....

Peerless.......................... ....

Harper's ....

In any quantities.

Finely Finished, and Tops Carpeted.

Commodes.

	Each.
No. 1. Black Walnut	**$4.00**
2. " "	**5.00**
3. " "	**6.00**

Complete with pan.

Blacking Cases.

No. 1. Black Walnut.... per doz., **$18.00**

Blacking Cases.

No. 2. Black Walnut....per doz., **$27.00**

Blacking Cases.

No. 3. Black Walnut....per doz., **$31.50**

Blacking Cases.

No. 5. Black Walnut.....per doz., **$18.00**

Blacking Cases.

No. 4. Black Walnut....per doz., **$36.00**

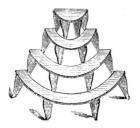

Flower Stands.

	Per doz.
Small Semi-circle, 3 shelf	**$12.60**
Large " 4 "	**21.60**
Corner........	**16.20**

Flower Stands.

	Per doz.
Small, Square, 3 shelf	**$12.60**
Large, " 4 "	**16.20**

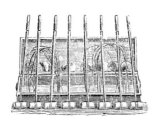

Croquet.

	Each.
¾ Set, Good Finish....	**$0.75**
Full Set, Plain Finish...	**75**
" Good "	**90**
" Design Mallets	**1.00**
" " "	**1.15**
" " "	**1.25**
" " "	**1.50**
" Professional Mallets	**2.50**

Chairs.

	Per doz.
Rattan, small sitting, with hole....	**$7.50**
" " " cane seat....	**7.50**
" " rocking	**7.50**
Willow Nursery...................	**9.00**
" " extra.............	**10.50**
Rattan, high, with hole..........	**13.50**
" " solid seat	**13.50**
" single arm, sitting, each	**3.00**
" " " rocking, each	**3.50**
" double " sitting, each	**4.25**
" " " rocking, each	**4.50**

Faucets.

CORK LINED.

ONLY FIRST QUALITY.

			Per doz.
No. 0,	6 in. long..........		**$0.44**
" 2,	7 in. "		**48**
" 4,	8 in. "		**60**
" 6,	9 in. "		**75**
" 8,	10 in. "		**90**
" 8½,	12 in. "		**1.60**
" 9,	18 in. " lager refr.......		**2.50**
" 9½,	24 in. " " "		**3.00**
" 10,	13¾ in. " ¾ bore..........		**3.25**
" 11,	15 in. " 1 " hhds		**3.75**
Brass, 9½ in. long			**24.00**
" 17 in. long..........			**36.00**
Lager Beer, Extension, 12 in........			**1.75**
" " " 16 in..... ..			**2.00**

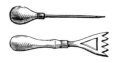

Ice Picks.

	Per doz.
No. 0, Awl......................	**$1.25**
" 1, "	**1.50**
Combination Tinned.	**1.75**
Ice Chisel........................	**3.25**

WOODENWARE SUNDRIES.

Back Rests.
Black Walnut .... per doz., **$18.00**

Bath Brick.
2 dozen in a box .... per box, **$0.90**

Blacking.
Bixby's Best, No. 1	...... Per doz.,	**$0.35**
"	" 2	"	**40**
"	" 3	"	**60**
"	" 4	"	**70**

Bread Boards.
Round, Plain........ ...Per doz., **$4.50**
" Fancy.......... " **6.00**

Chopping Knives.
No. 1 .... Per doz., **$2.25**
" 2 .... " **3.75**
" 3 .... " **5.50**
" 4 .... " **3.25**

Clothes Pins.
Per Box, 5 gross, full count........ **$0.75**
Ball's Patent.... . .....Per gross, **1.10**
Smith's " .... " **1.40**

Clothes Poles.
Pine ....Per doz., **$2.25**

Coffee Mills.
Per doz.
No. 4, Iron Hopper **$5.00**
" 104, " **8.50**
" 102, " **9.00**
" 70, " Side Mill **10.00**
" 108, Britannia Hopper **11.00**
" 106, " **12.00**
" 301, French............ ....**13.00**
Discount, 45 per cent.

Drip Pans for Refrigerators.
No. 1, Galvanized Iron ...Per doz., **$4.50**

Hammocks.
Mexican Grass, full size,
White..............Per doz., **$19.00**
Colored .... " **20.00**

Mouse Traps.
Common, 1 to 6 Holes, per dozen
Holes... ... ...**$0.18**
Delusion ....Per doz., **1.50**
Wheel .... " **2.00**

Mallets.
Per doz.
No. 108, Hickory, Tinner's........**$0.90**
" 107, " " **1.10**
" 45, " Carpenter's...... **1.25**
" 1, " " **2.25**
" 43, " " **2.75**
" 51, Lignum Vitæ, Small..... **3.00**
" 49, " Large...... **5.00**
" 48, Hickory, Iron-bound...... **6.50**

Mops.
6 lb......... ... .Per doz., **$1.30**
9 lb..................... " **2.00**
12 lb .... " **2.50**
Dish Mops, Common .... " **85**
" Extra **1.00**
" " Fancy.... ....**1.15**

Pulley Blocks.
Small ....Per doz,, **$0.70**
Large .... " **80**

Shaker Swifts.
Small................ ...Per doz., **$10.50**
Medium .. .. " **11.25**
Large .... " **12.00**

Slaw Cutters.
1 Knife ....Per doz., **$3.00**
2 Knives................ " **5.00**
Vegetable Cutters........ " **2.00**

Soap Cups.
5 inch ....Per doz., **$0.60**
6 " .... " **70**
7 " .... " **80**

Toothpicks.
Double pointed, 2,500 in a Box,
Per doz. boxes, **$0.75**

Wardrobe Strips.
Pine, 2½ in. wide.... .....Per foot, **$0.02**
Black Walnut, 2½ in. wide, " **4**

Well Buckets.
Per doz.
Light, Plain Iron Hoops and Straps,**$4.00**
No. 1, " " " " **5.50**
Light, Galv'd " " " **5.50**
No. 1, " " " " **7.25**

Doll Carriages.

Per doz.

No.   0, as per cut................$7.00
"   110, Bow Top, 4 wheel 6.50
"   104,   "   "   Large, 4 wheel..   9.00

Doll Carriages.

Per doz.

No. 111, As per cut...............$6.50
"   0, 3 Wheel, Canopy.... .....   7.00

Doll Carriages.

Per doz.

No. 103, As per cut, the best Doll
     Carriage, in the market
     for price. $9.00
"   3, Canopy,   Movable   Top,
     Upholstered 15.00
"   3½, Same as No. 3, Upholstered
     with Reps.............18.00
"   4, Canopy,   Movable   Top,
     Phaeton   Body,   Raised
     Panels, Upholstered with
     Reps 24.00
"   5, Same as No. 4, Extra Finish
     Oval Tire... ....33.00

Doll Carriages.

Per doz.

No. 105, New Style, Slat Body,
     Painted and Ornament-
     ed, Movable Top, as No.
     103 ....$12.00
"   107, As per cut, with Movable
     Top, Finely Painted and
     Ornamented 15.00

Doll Carriages.

Per doz.

Small Willow Body..... ....$9.00
Large   "   " 12.00
No. 112, Rattan Body, Canopy Top.27.00
"   113,   "   "   Parasol "   .30.00

Doll Carriages.

Per doz.

No. 118, As per cut, Finely Uphol-
     stered,   Painted,   and
     Ornamented. $30.00
"   119, As per cut, Upholstered
     with Silk or Satin.....   36.00

Skeleton Wagon with Team.

Per doz.

23 inches long, as per cut **$3.00**

Barrel Wagon.

Per doz.

7 inches long, containing ten pins..**$1.25**

Toy Wagons.

Per doz.

Daisy, 6¼x3½ inches................**$0.40**
Whoa Emma, 5x9 inches, painted,
    assorted colors, and lettered...... **75**

Painted Wagons.

Per doz.

No. 151, Body 7x15, as per cut, Var-
        nished Gearing.........**$3.50**
 "   152, Body 8x16, Varnished Gear-
        ing.......... ....**4.00**

Boys' Wagons.

Varnished, Ornamented, and Lettered. Front Wheels Turn Under Body.   Per doz.

Boss.	Body 8x16,	Straight Wood Axles..................... ....**$4.00**
No. 155,	"	11x22,	"	"	"	**7.50**
" 156,	"	13x26, Curved	"	"	with seat........................	**9.00**
" 157,	"	13x26,	"	Iron	" " "	**15.00**
" 80,	"	12x24, Straight	"	"	Braced Handle......................	**14.00**
" 82,	"	13x26,	"	"	" " "	**16.00**
" 84,	"	14x28,	"	"	" " "	**19.00**
" 86,	"	15x32,	"	"	" " "	**21.00**
Seats for Nos. 80 and 82.....................................						**1.75**
" " " 84 and 86..................						**3.00**

Body Painted, Ornamented, and Lettered. Front Wheels Turn Under.

No. 81,	Body 12x24,	Straight Iron Axles, with seat............. ....**18.00**
" 83,	"	13x26,	"	"	"	" "	**20.00**
" 85,	"	14x28,	"	"	"	" "	**25.50**
" 87,	"	15x32,	"	"	"	" "	**27.50**
" 168,	"	17x40,	"	"	"	" " " Braced Handle, with Shaft
		and Two-Seats, Welded Tire, Frame Body, for Dog or Goat.........**60.00**

Shafts for Wagons, assorted sizes............................... .... **9.00**

Toy Carts.

			Per doz.
No.	0.	6 x10½, Painted, Com....	**$1.25**
"	13.	5 x10, Ex., with Tin Tires	**1.75**
"	14.	7 x12, " " " "	**2.25**
"	15.	7¾x14, " " " "	**3.00**
"	12.	6½x11, Flaring Tin Tires, with Rest under Tongue	**2.25**
"	11.	7½x13, Flaring Tin Tires, with Rest under Tongue	**3.00**
"	3.	6 x10½, Var. Iron Wheel..	**3.00**
"	4.	7 x11, Skel. " "	**3.25**
"	5.	7 x11, " Wood "	**3.25**
"	6.	9½x17, Varnished "	**7.00**
"	7.	11x20, " "	**9.00**

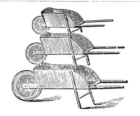

Wheelbarrows.

			Per doz.
No. 0,	24 inch Handles, Plain.....		**$2.25**
" 1,	24 " " Varnished		**2.75**
" 2,	24 " " Painted..		**3.00**
" 3,	Nested, 3 sizes, 27, 31, 35 inch Handles, Varnished..		**4.00**
" 4,	Nested, 3 sizes, 27, 31, 35 inch Handles, Painted....		**4.50**
" 5,	9 inch Spoke Wheel, Var..		**5.00**
" 6,	11 " " " " ..		**9.00**
" 7,	11 " " " Paint.		**10.00**
" 8,	13 " " " "		**.18.00**

Boys' Propellers.

		Each.
No. 1, Small	....	**$3.00**
" 2, Large	....	**3.25**

Girls' Propellers.

	Each.
No. 1......	**$4.50**
" 2..........................	**5.00**
" 3..........................	**5.50**

Velocipedes.

				Each.
No. 0,	Front Wheel, 13 inches.....			**$3.00**
" 1,	" " 18 "			**3.25**
" 2,	" " 22 "			**3.75**
" 3,	" " 25 "			**4.25**
" 4,	" " 27 "			**4.75**

Bicycles.

				Each.
No. 1,	Front Wheel, 28 inches.....			**$7.00**
" 2,	" " 32 "			**9.00**
" 3,	" " 36 "			**15.00**
" 4,	" " 42 "			**20.00**

Discount, 20 per cent.

Chair Rockers.

Each.

No. 1, Painted and Ornamented....**$0.65**

Infant Rockers.

Each.

No. 1, Painted and Ornamented.... **$0.75**
" 2, " 2 Heads.... ...... **1.25**
" 3, Walnut Carpeted.......... **1.75**
" 4 " " 2 Heads.... **2.00**

Dexter Rockers.

Each.

No. 1, Plain...................... **$0.65**
" 2, Upholstered............... **75**

Shoo Fly Rockers.

Each.

No. 1, Small, Enameled........... **$1.25**
" 2, Large, " **1.50**
" 3, Small, Rep Lined **1.75**
" 4, Large, " " **2.00**

Rocking Horses.

Each.

No. 0, Thug, 4½ inch Block, Painted
 Mane, no Stirrups........ **$0.65**
" 0½, Thug, 5 inch Block, Painted
 Mane, no Stirrups........ **75**
" 1, Thug, 5 inch Block, Larger,
 Hair Mane and Stirrups... **1.00**
" 2, Thug, 6 inch Block, Hair
 Mane and Stirrups........ **1.25**
" 2½, Thug, 7 inch Block, Hair
 Mane and Stirrups.... ... **2.00**
" 3, Hobby, 6 inch Block, Hair
 Mane and Regular Saddle. **1.75**

Saddle Horses.

Each.

No. 4. 6 inch Block, Carved Legs.. **$2.65**
" 5. 7 " " " " .. **3.35**
" 6. 8 " " " " .. **4.25**
" 7. 10 " " " " .. **6.00**

Platform Horses.

Per doz.

No. 1, 10 inches high..............$4.50
"   2, 11½   "   " 5.50
"   3, 14   "   " 7.50
"   4, 16   "   " 9.00
"   5, 19   "   " 13.50
"   6, 19   "   "   Ex. finish and
                       Saddle.....15.00

On Finely Ornamented Platforms, with
   Iron Axles and Wheels.

Spring Horses.

Each.

No. 1, Small 7 inch Block.........$7.50
"   2, Medium 8 "   " 9.50
"   3, Large 10 "   " 12.00

Finely finished.

Toy Cribs.

FANCY PAINTED.

Per doz.

No. 1, 7x14... ... .$2.50
"   2, 10x20...................... 4.00
"   3, 12x25.......... .   ... 5.00

Patent Folding Toy Crib.

Per doz.

22 inches long, 10 inches wide, 13
   inches high......... ....$9.00

Toy Bedsteads.

Per doz.

Painted, Assorted Colors, 3 in a
   Nest, 16, 20, 24 inches long.......$3.75

Toy Bedstead.

Style as per cut, Light Hardwood,
   Varnished.

Per doz.

No. 1, 20 inches long..............$4.50
"   2, 24   "   " 6.00

Toy Painted Chairs.

Per doz.

No. 1, Small Sitting Seat, 4x4......**$1.15**
" 2, " Rocking Seat, 4x4.... **1.25**
" 3, Medium Sitting, 5½x5½ **1.75**
" 4, " Rocking. 5½x5½.... **2.00**
" 5, Large Sitting, 9x9. .... **3.50**
" 6, " " 11x11. ...... **4.50**
" 7, " Rocking, 11x11........ **5.50**

Gem.

Per doz.

Toy Painted Chair, as per cut,
Height, 19 inches; width of Seat,
10 inches; Handsomely Painted..**$4.50**
1776, Toy Painted Chair, height. 16
inches; width of seat, 10 inches;
hard wood, cane seat, and handsomely painted.................. **3.50**

Toy Bureaus.

PAINTED BRIGHT FANCY COLORS.

Per doz.

No. 5, 15x15, 3 Drawers...........**$9.00**
" 6, 18x18, 3 Drawers **12.00**

Toy Painted Arm Chairs.

Per doz.

No. 1, Small, 5x5¼........ ..... .**$1.75**
" 2, Large, 9x10.......... .... **3.75**
" 3, " Rocking, 9x10 ...... **4.25**

Excelsior Chairs.

Per doz.

Hardwood, Varnished, Light and
Dark, Wood Seat and Back, size
of Seat, 10x13, as per cut.......**$9.00**
Same as above, without Rockers... **8.50**

Toy Bureaus.

Style as per cut, Light Hardwood,
Varnished.

Per doz.

No. 1, 2 Drawers, Height 14 in.. **$6.00**
" 2, 2 " " 17½ in.. **9.00**
" 3, 3 " " 22 in.. **12.00**
Style Queen Anne, Bl'k Wal't.
A, 2 Drawers, Height, 23 in..**$21.00**
B, 3 " " 28 in.. **27.00**

Toy Desk.
Per doz.
Made of Light Hardwood, Varnished, Lid to raise **$9.00**
18 inches long, 14½ inches wide, 25 inches high.

Boys' Office Desk.
Per doz.
Made of Light Hardwood, Varnished, with 6 Drawers; Lid to raise.........................**$30.00**
24 inches long, 14 inches wide, 26 inches high.

Toy Sideboard.
Per doz.
Style as per cut, Light Hardwood, Varnished, length, 11 inches, height, 14 inches.... . ...**$9.00**

Blackboard.
Ash Frame.............Per doz., **$9.00**
24 by 30 inches.

Toy Painted Table.
Per doz.
No. 1, Size 23x15x14..............**$7.50**
" 2, As per cut, elegantly painted in new style, Drawer containing Alphabet Blocks; length, 24 inches; height, 17 inches................ **9.00**

Toy Extension Table.
Per doz.
Hardwood, Imitation of Black Walnut, 36 inches long, when extended................ ....**$18.00**
Black Walnut, as per cut........ **30.00**

Toy Leaf Table.
Per doz.
Hardwood, Imitation of Black Walnut, 30 inches long, 23½ inches wide, 19 inches high.....**$15.00**

Toy Pails.

			Per doz.
No. 1, Infant's,		Painted	$0.50
" 2,	"	Ornamented	55
" 3,	"	Brass Bound	65
" 4, Toy,		Painted	55
" 5,	"	Ornamented	60
" 6,	"	Brass Bound	70
" 7,	¼	Painted	1.00
" 8,	¼	Ornamented	1.10
" 9,	¼	Brass Bound	1.15

Toy Cedar Tubs.

Brass Hoops, 3 Sizes, Assorted.

	Per doz.
No. 1, Plain	$2.25
" 2, Striped	2.75

Toy Zinc Washboards.

	Per doz.
No. 1, Small, 6 inch	$0.40
" 2, Medium, 8 inch	50
" 3, Large, 10 inch	65
" 4, " 12 "	85

Boys' Tool Chests.

				Per doz.
No. 33,	13 Assorted Articles			$1.50
" 22,	8	"	Tools	1.50
" 122,	9	"	"	1.75
" 44,	12	"	"	2.25
" 55,	18	"	"	4.50
" 66,	23	"	"	7.00
" 77,	25	"	"	9.00
" 2050,	18	"	"	7.50
" 105,	25	"	"	8.50
" 1050,	25	"	"	12.00
Pioneer,	26	"	"	15.00
Champion,	28	"	"	18.00
Hero	31	"	"	27.00
No. 0,	45	"	"	48.00
" 0½,	51	"	"	60.00

Log Cabin Building Blocks.

Hardwood, finely finished, 10 inches long, 10 inches wide, 13 inches high, packed in a Wood Box...............per doz., $9.00

American Toy Drums.

BEST QUALITY.

			Per doz.
No. 0,	5 inches diameter	....	**$3.00**
" 1,	6 " "	....	**3.75**
" 2,	7 " "	....	**4.50**
" 3,	8 " "	....	**6.00**
" 4,	9 " "	....	**7.50**
" 5,	10 " "	....	**9.00**
" 6,	11 " "	....	**10.50**
" 7,	12 " "	....	**15.00**
" 8,	13 " "	....	**18.00**
" 9,	15 " "	....	**24.00**

Discount, **40** per cent.

Metal Drums.

ALL BRASS COLOR.

				Per doz.
No, 0,	5 in. Diam., Cord Fast'g	....	**$2.00**
" 1,	8 " " " "	....	**4.00**
" 2,	9 " " " "	....	**5.00**
" 3,	10 " " " "	....	**6.50**
" 4,	11 " " " "	....	**7.50**
" 5,	12 " " " "	....	**8.50**
" 6,	13 " " " "	....	**9.00**
" 1,	8 " " Rod "	....	**4.50**
" 5,	12 " " " "	...	**9.00**
Six in a set	.... " "	...	**4.50**

Net, no discount.

Children's Rolling Hoops.

NO.	KIND.	SIZES.	SMALLEST.	LARGEST.	PER GROSS.	
1	Chestnut.	12	22 inches.	30 inches.	With Drivers,	**$4.50**
2	Oak.	18	22 "	36 "	" "	**6.50**
3	Oak, round edge.	18	22 "	36 "	" "	**7.50**
4	Ash.	12	26 "	34 "	" "	**9.00**
5	"	18	24 "	40 "	" "	**10.50**
6	Round, painted, with Iron Tire.	6	28 "	34 "	" "	**30.00**

Chime Rolling Hoops, 12 inch Wheel...... ... .Per doz., **$3.75**
" " " 20 " " .... " **4.00**

Children's Jumping Ropes.

No. 1, Jute Rope, plain handles......................	Per gross,	**$3.00**
" 2, " " fancy " longer	"	**4.00**
" 3, " " " " "	"	**6.00**
" 4, " " " " extra long....	"	**9.00**
" 5, " " " " double length.......................	"	**12.00**
" 6, Fancy " " " small...............................	"	**4.50**
" 7, " " " " medium...........................	"	**7.50**
" 8, " " " " large.............................	"	**12.00**

Toy Reins.

	Per doz.
No. 1, With Bells..................	**$1.00**
" 2, " " and Bugles........	**2.00**
" 3, " " extra............	**2.50**

Toy Chamber Sets.

	Per doz. Sets.
Six Pieces, Painted	**$13.50**
Seven Pieces. Painted, Larger....	**21.00**
Light Hard Wood, Varnished....	**21.00**

Children's Swings.

			Per doz.
No.	1,	Upholstered, Enameled Cloth..............	**$7.50**
	2,	Upholstered, Carpet......	**9.00**
	3,	Black Walnut, Upholstered, Fancy Cloth.....	**9.00**
"	4,	Oak, Varnished Extra, Chair Seat Style.......	**12.00**

Mats for Children's Carriages.

IN BRIGHT, FANCY COLORS.

Per doz.

No. 1, Size 10x12, Wool Cloth, assorted colors.................................**$3.50**
" 2, " 11x12, " star centres............................ . . .... **4.00**
" 3, " 8x 8, Long Wool, assorted colors.................... .. .... **6.00**
" 4, " 9x 9, " " " **7.00**
" 5, " 10x10, " " " **8.50**
" 6, " 11x11, All-wool, fancy centres and borders.... .... **9.00**

Afghans in great variety...................... ....from **$9.00** to **$48.00** per doz.

Carriage straps........... ....**$1.00** " "

CHILDREN'S CARRIAGES.

Discount, 25 per cent.

All Willow and Rattan Carriages finished on natural Wood.

All the different parts of our Children's Carriages constantly on hand.

No. 42.

A four-bow, open side carriage, with steel springs, iron axles, round-tired wheels, single joints, and upholstered with enameled cloth neatly painted and finished.

Price................................. ....**$6.50**

No. 43.

New style phaeton body with raised dasher, as per cut, upholstered with enameled cloth, oil-cloth mat, covered bows, curtains, round tired, tapering spoke wheels.

Price........ ....**$7.50**

No. 44.

New style phaeton body, raised dasher, full-side springs, as per cut, upholstered with terry, carpet mat, covered bows, plated joints, tapering spoked wheels, finely finished.

Price..................................... .... **$9.50**

No. 45.

Similar to above, with painted panels, upholstered in coteline, stuffed top, double-plated joints, etc., handsomely finished.

Price... ....**$12.00**

No. 46.

New style phaeton body, with raised panels, full side springs, as per cut, uphol-stered in worsted coteline, carpet mat, head lining, fringed curtain, tubular bows, socket handle. Very handsomely finished.

Price..**$14.00**

No. 1.

New style of cheap carriage, unexcelled in price. Body twenty-nine inches long, sixteen and twenty-inch wheels, wood finish, wood axles, painted inside.

Price................................ ....**$4.50**

No. 2.

Same as No. 1, upholstered with enamel cloth, iron axles.

Price.......... ....**$5.00**

No. 3.

Same as No. 1, but with iron axles and steel springs, upholstered with mosaic.

Price... .... **$5.50**

No. 31

Cut under body, with straight back and spindle front, four independent springs with reach, upholstered with mosaic, and bullion fringe scallop curtains and outside curtains.

Price..$10.50

No. 32.

Same as No. 31, upholstered in cretone or jute, tapestry mat

Price..$11.50

No. 33.

Phaeton body with spindle front, on springs front and back, with reach, on iron axles, upholstered in jutes, tapestry mat, bullion fringe curtains and outside curtains, as per cut.

Price..$12.00

No. 34.

Same as No. 33, but trimmed with ramie, Brussels mat, full-plated trimmings.

Price..$13.00

No. 53.

Style of body and gearing represented by above cut, upholstered in enameled cloth, oil-cloth mat, outside curtains, round tired, tapering [spoke wheels. The cheapest canopy carriage in the market.

Price.... ....**$9.00**

No. 54.

Has the new style phaeton body like No. 55, raised dasher and gearing, upholstered in terry, carpet mat, outside curtains, side rails, tipped handle, round tired, tapering spoke wheels. Handsomely painted and ornamented.

Price..... ....**$10.50**

No. 55.

Style of body and gearing represented by above cut, upholstered with coteline, roll back, carpet mat, outside curtains, side rails, tipped handles, round tired, tapering spoke wheels, painted panels.

Price **$12.00**

No. 56.

Same style as represented above; upholstered in worsted coteline points and rolls, raised panels, socket handles. Handsomely finished throughout.

Price....... ....**$14.00**

No. 57.

Style of body and gearing represented by above cut, except rail and head rest; upholstered throughout with rep, oil-cloth mat, curtains, etc. A good, substantial carriage.

Price.... ....**$12.00**

No. 58.

Same style as represented by above cut, with quarter rail, upholstered with good rep, carpet mat, curtains, etc. Finely finished.

Price..**$15.00**

No. 59.

Style of body and gearing represented by above cut, half rail, upholstering of coteline, carpet mat, curtains, etc. Handsomely finished body and gearing.

Price..**$18.00**

No. 60.

Style of body and gearing as represented by above cut, full rail, upholstered with French silk coteline, velvet mat, curtains, etc. Elegantly finished throughout.

Price..**$21.00**

No. 24.

Style of body and gearing represented by above cut, hardwood spindles fitted into a wood frame body, varnished on the natural wood, gearing painted to match; upholstered with wool, terry or Russian tapestry, full length Brussels carpet, front rail only.

Price..**$17.00**

No. 25.

Similar to above in construction, and finished in the natural wood. Upholstered with satine or fine carriage cloth, in rolls. Canopy top with festoons and silk fringe to match, plated rails for front and back.

Price..**$20.00**

No. 27.

Constructed similar to numbers 24 and 25, except having a drop in centre of body; elegantly finished in natural wood color. Upholstered with silk in rolls, fine canopy top with heavy silk-fringed festoons, full length Brussels carpet, plated front and back rails, flat spoke wheels.

Price..**$25.00**

No. .03.

A stout, well-made, willow body. Continuous handle running gear, as per cut. Cushions of Cretonne, for seat and back, Brussels carpet, gingham parasol top.

Price:..**$10.00**

No. 5.

Fine willow body on side spring gearing, as per page 59. Upholstered at the sides as well as in the back with fancy goods or Union terry, has Brussels carpet the full length of the body, and is furnished with a parasol of Regina or Italian cloth.

Price..**$13.50**

No. 6.

Rattan body, style of above cut, except with straight bottom mounted on S springs. Upholstered with fancy Russian tapestry, carpeted its full length with Brussels carpet; has a parasol top of Regina or Italian cloth, *not fringed.*

Price... .**$15.00**

No. 06.

Rattan body, style, gearing and top represented by above cut. Upholstered with fancy imported goods, and has a Brussels carpet; has a parasol top of Regina or Italian cloth with pinked edges.

Price... ....**$16.00**

No. 7.

Style of body as per cut, of fine rattan, gearing style of No. 24, page 59. Upholstered with fine Russian tapestry, and has a Brussels carpet the entire length of the body. The parasol is of silk, lined and pinked.

Price..**$22.00**

No. 10.

Style of body and gearing represented by above cut. The body is formed of fine rattan work woven into a strongly made wooden frame, making a beautiful and comfortable shape. Upholstered with fine terry or with Russian tapestry, plated guard rail for front only. A carriage of rare beauty.

Price........................ ....**$18.00**

No. 82.

Wood frame body with fine rattan panels in ornamental patterns, finished wood color, springs as shown in cut.   Upholstered with fine ramie goods, fringe curtains, and outside curtains.

Price..**$21.00**

No. 83.

Upholstered with silk damask, chenille fringe top, Brussels mat, beautifully finished in all particulars.

Price..**$24.00**

No. 29.

Rattan body, style as per cut, of woven cane, star pattern, with cane ring ribbon border. Its length and depth make it a decidedly comfortable and cozy carriage, especially for an infant child. Is upholstered with fancy imported goods of heavy texture and attractive colors, with roll or puffing to match. The parasol is of Regina or Italian cloth, pinked. Brussels carpet full length of body.

Price............................... ....**$20.00**

No. 9.

Style of body and gearing as per cut. The body has one more row of rings at the side than this illustration shows, giving it more depth. The body is made of pure cane, worked into an elegant ring and star pattern design, upholstered with French figured natural silk in colors, in rolls and puffs, rich Brussels carpet, full length of body. Silk parasol, lined and pinked.

Price **$25.00**

No. 032.

Style as per cut, with a fine rattan body, braided in star pattern, with ribbon border of woven ring work. Dash and back finished in diamond pattern cane, upholstered in rolls with velvet puffing. The parasol is of rich silk, lined and handsomely fringed, all the colors harmonizing. The running gear is finished in a superior manner, mounted on *Flat-Spoked Wheels.*

Price..$30.00

No. 35.

Style as per cut. The body of this carriage is of fine cane, woven in star pattern, with border and wheel guards, of wound cane and ring work all of the best workmanship, upholstered with silk in rolls, bordered by a puffing of plush to match. The parasol is of silk, on square frame, heavily fringed. Velvet carpet.

Price.. ....**$35.00**

No. 36.

Style of above, upholstered with heavy satin, with silk plush puffing. The parasol is of satin, elegantly fringed. The hub caps, handle tips, springs, and parasol rod are nickel-plated. Velvet carpet. This is as fine a carriage as can be made. No pains will be spared to have it suited to the most refined taste.

Price.. ....**$50.00**

TWIN CARRIAGE.

No. 4.

New style phaeton body, raised dasher, painted panels, full side springs, as per cut, upholstered with coteline, stuffed top, double-plated joints, etc.   Handsomely finished; extra strong, suitable for twins.

Price **$20.00**

No. 5.

Canopy Top, as per cut of No. 55, page 56.

New style phaeton body, raised dasher with gearing, as represented by cut, upholstered with coteline, roll back, carpet mat, curtains, side rails, tipped handles, etc. Handsomely finished, extra strong, suitable for twins.

Price...**$24.00**

Dear Sir:

This Catalogue is respectfully presented to solicit your orders.

F. S. GWYER, }
L. H. MACE. }

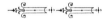

⇥ T E R M S : ⇤

NET CASH IN THIRTY DAYS.

All Accounts Subject to Draft at Sight after Thirty Days.

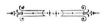

NOTICE.

Prices subject to change without notice.

All goods packed closely, in the most secure manner; the boxing charged at cost.

No charge for carting or shipping goods.

All dimensions given are the extreme outside.

L. H. MACE AND COMPANY
an historical introduction

Of all items to be found in the American home, woodenware has changed the least. Although the mechanics of producing this product have grown more complex and sophisticated since the mid-nineteenth century, the functional design and utility of the material has remained constant. Housewives today will recognize some of the same utensils which they use for preparation or storage of food in the 1883 wholesale catalog of L. H. Mace and Co., a New York merchant.

Levi H. Mace was a carpenter and founded the woodenware and refrigerator business in 1850. It was first located on Allen Street in lower Manhattan, but in 1854 the business was moved to East Houston Street. L. H. Mace was to remain at 111, 113, 115 and 117 East Houston in the building pictured on the catalog's title page until the early 1900's. It served as the company's manufacturing plant and showrooms, as well as providing warehouse space. In the 1890's the firm established an additional warehouse in the Bronx on East 150th St., near River Avenue.

Mace was one of many small manufacturing companies to disappear in the Depression days of the 1930's. Wooden refrigerators were the firm's staple item, and by 1930 technology had caught up with them. Woodenware sundries and children's carriages constructed of wood were still in demand at the time, but these products, as well, were declining in popularity.

Little or no record is left of the firm's general history. It is clear, however, that Levi Mace was the principal figure in the business until the turn-of-the-century. Presumably, he died in the early 1900's. The 1908–09 New York City Directory carries a listing for Levi H. Mace (estate of), at 3832 White Plains Road, the Bronx. Succeeding him as president was Arthur I. Mace, perhaps his son. In 1915–16 Arthur Mace was listed in the City Directory as president and John L. Gwyer, vice–president. The latter was most probably a relative, if not the son, of F. S. Gwyer whose name appears along with that of Levi Mace in the 1883 catalog. By 1915, the company had left its imposing East Houston Street building for an office at 15–17 East 32nd Street. By 1933 the firm had disappeared from the New York city business directory and from the telephone book. In 1937, the *Marvin Scudder Manual of Extinct or Obsolete Companies* listed it as being out of business.

Levi Mace seems to have begun his business primarily as a wooden refrigerator maker. He is so listed in the 1852 New York City Directory.

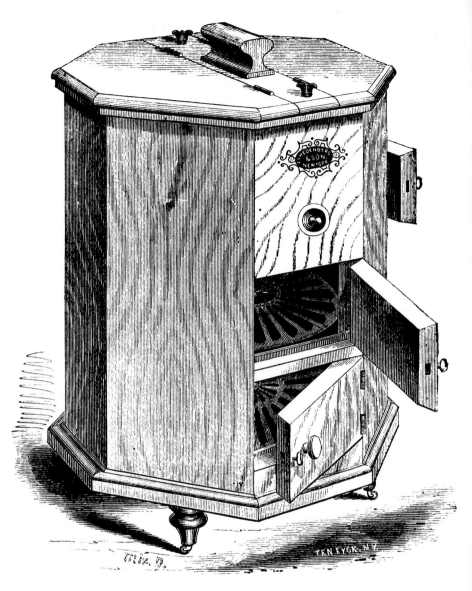

Octagonal icebox. From the F. L. Hendenberg & Son, New York, N.Y., catalog, c. 1880.—*New York Historical Society*

The first primitive refrigerator was patented in England in 1834 by an American, Jacob Perkins. In 1850, when Mace started in business, artificial methods of producing ice were being introduced. No longer was an icehouse necessary for the storage of the frozen substance, or a springhouse needed for the proper handling of perishables. It is said that the wood icebox—called by most manufacturers a refrigerator—was one of the first great additions to the farm kitchen after the iron range. It was an especially useful item for the urban home and business.

Although the lathe has been known since the thirteenth century, more sophisticated instruments for the turning of complicated shapes and forms were not available until the invention of the gunstock lathe in 1820. This machine still required the attention of a helper who turned the object by hand and an operator who applied the cutters. A lathe with a foot treadle, however, was introduced in the mid-nineteenth century, and greatly expedited the production of wares. Factory production of woodenware superseded home production in the 1850's in small shops and plants across the country. L. H. Mace had such strong competitors in the woodenware business as F. A. Walker and Co., and Lincoln and Hopkinson, of Boston, the Van Heusen-Charles Company of Albany, N.Y., and John G. Koehler of Philadelphia; and in the refrigerator line by three New York makers, Alex M. Lesley, William Laws, and Hedenberg & Sons, and others in Boston, Cincinnati, Minneapolis, and Grand Rapids, Mich. Children's carriage makers were legion, especially in New England.

Woodenware was, of course, available in a thousand-and-one house-wares' catalogs, general and hardware stores, and from peddlers. Mace must have done the bulk of its business wholesale through jobbers and dealers. Before the advent of factory production, an expert on early American woodenware, Mary Earle Gould, has written, "each family produced its own utensils from the wood lying at hand, and when worn out new ones were whittled and perhaps made a bit more satisfactory than the old." The factory items were often not as beautifully crafted as the handhewn, but in the plastic world of today when wood in the form of bowls and spoons is highly valued, these early factory products are rightly considered collectors' items. Also known as "treen-ware" (*tree-ware*), they are highly sought by museums. Very early handhewn woodenware is almost impossible to come by. It was most often discarded when well-used. The fact that wood products were "turned" on a lathe does not lessen their value as art objects. The manufacture of woodenware, unlike that of stamped or moulded objects, was and has remained a craft. In the hands of a skilled lathe operator, it was an art.

Among the first items produced in the factories were the round nest of boxes. Nest boxes (illustrated on page 30 of the catalog) were used for the storing of spices, and were available in a variety of different woods. Shaker and Amish craftsmen produced the best known of these items in their shops. Constructed of wood strips that had been made pliable in hot water, these pieces of wood were shaped around a mould, folded over, and then fastened. Small nails were used to attach the strips, a bottom and a lid. Wood containers had been used for the storage of other foodstuffs such as meal, flour, sugar and coffee until the 1840's, but they were replaced by the tin cannister and bin. Wooden spice chests and salt boxes became popular items in the late 1800's. Even today, many housewives have an abhorrence of metal containers and cooking spoons.

The most common woods used by Mace and other companies of the time were pine, ash and black walnut. These were cheaper and easier to use than such early common woods as maple, beech, cherry and sycamore. Some pine products were given an "imitation oak" or "imitation granite" painting. Mace produced a number of its refrigerators in this manner.

Among the household sundries the company offered are some of the most sought-after collectors' items today: butler's trays, knife trays, settee tables (also known as "folding ironing tables"), churns, butter moulds and prints, measures, salt boxes, commodes, blacking cases, coffee mills and lap boards. No self-respecting nineteenth-century middle-class housewife would have been without most of them.

Fewer, however, would have possessed one of the fifteen refrigerator models which Mace patented and manufactured. A great variety were available—for the nursery, upright and chest refrigerators for the home, and grocers', lager beer, and restaurant models. Nearly all were fairly simple in construction and easy to use. The most expensive were manufactured from ash; the simpler models were made of pine with imitation oak painting. "Excelsior" and "Diamond" models were made for the home and were available at prices as low as $2.75 for a 25″ x 18″ x 24″ chest model to as high as $56 for a 57″ x 30″ x 63″ upright model. For most effective cooling, it is said that the chest refrigerator was to be preferred, but more upright models were offered. Along with the refrigerators, Mace offered a recently patented "Excelsior" water tank for storing ice water in any of the upright home models. It could be purchased for $1.50, and produced more frigid drinking water than the water cooler. Perhaps Europeans should blame Mace for the American addiction to ice water.

In contrast to other refrigerators on the market, Mace did not offer models with special linings of porcelain or cork. Shelves were made of zinc and linings were of the same material or of galvanized iron. Most of these refrigerators would hold ninety to one-hundred pounds of ice, and a twenty-five pound block could be expected to last at least one day.

The other refrigeration items were of the same simple design. Meat safes and ice cream freezers were utilitarian in every respect. A patent for an ice cream freezer was first issued in 1848, and by the 1880's everyone wanted to have a freezer. Mace offered some "Good, reliable and cheap" models as well as the "Celebrated Triple Motion White Mountain Freezer" manufactured by the White Mountain Freezer Company of Nashua, N.H. Only the water coolers carried any kind of decoration. According to the catalog, they were "Ornamented with Bouquets, Landscapes, Etc."

Among the more interesting items carried by Mace were wooden toys. Some of them may have been manufactured from scrap lumber in the East Houston Street plant, but a majority were probably imported. A child could choose a chair rocker, a Dexter rocker, a shoo-fly rocker, a regular rocking horse, a saddle horse rocker, a platform horse, or a spring horse. Boys could select from wagons, propellers, velocipedes, bicycles, tool chests, building blocks and drums. Girls had a complete set of home furnishings— cribs, bedsteads, chairs, bureaus, desks, tables, and wash tubs. Some were the proper size for a doll house; others were suitable as furniture for a

Baby carriage with parasol. From the Tallman Toy Co., New York, N.Y., 1892 illustrated catalog of baby's carriages.—*New York Historical Society*

children's play room. The three-foot long black walnut "Toy Extension Table" (page 46), costing $2.50 wholesale, is a particularly novel item. A parent today would probably want it as a coffee table.

Among the most beautiful and finely made of Mace's merchandise were the children's carriages. Some cheap models were available, but most were fairly expensive, the better ones ranging in price from $25 to $50. Some of the them were designed along the lines of the adult phaeton carriage. Others were based on classic baby carriage models. The natural wood, rattan and willow carriages are especially attractive. A few were carpeted in velvet, upholstered in silk, and sported silk parasols. A nursemaid or mother could take the baby out in great style in such a fancy carriage. Unlike some modern models, they were light and easy to maneuver.

It is unfortunate that such a company as Mace failed to survive the difficult days of the 1930's. A market for fine wood products certainly exists today. Such a utilitarian item as the icebox has enjoyed its day, but the natural medium of wood has and will again provide useful and aesthetically pleasing household articles. Those who are fortunate enough to find such items as those manufactured by Mace will possess truly functional antiques.

Suggestions for further reading

Literature on factory-produced woodenware is almost non-existent. Readers interested in the subject, however, will find that books on early woodenware provide useful information on the types of items which have been available in America for several hundred years; these volumes also supply the reader with general information on early manufacturing methods.

GOULD, MARY EARLE. *The Early American House.* Rutland, Vt.: Charles E. Tuttle Co., 1965.
GOULD, MARY EARLE. *Early American Wooden Ware.* Rutland, Vt.: Charles E. Tuttle Co., 1962.
LANTZ, LOUIS K. *Old American Kitchenware, 1725–1925.* Published jointly by Thomas Nelson, Inc., Camden and New York, and Everybodys Press, Hanover, Penn., 1970.

other trade catalogs

F. A. WALKER & CO., Boston, Mass.; 1871–1875 catalogs of useful and ornamental goods for the home. The 1871 catalog of 130 pages is available at the Metropolitan Museum, New York, N.Y., and the Metro-Goldwyn-Mayer Archives, Culver City, Calif. The 1872 catalog is available from the Ford Motor Co. Archives at Greenfield Village, Dearborn, Mich., and from the New York State Library, Albany, N.Y. It is an 106-page illustrated catalog. The 1875 catalog amounts to only 10 pages and is found in the New York State Library, Albany.

WHITE MOUNTAIN FREEZER CO., Nashua, N.H.; 1890–91 catalogs of ice cream freezers. Available from either the New Hampshire Historical Society, Concord, or from the Minnesota Historical Society, St. Paul.

WHEATON & HICKOX, Worcester, Mass.; c. 1845 catalog of everything for the home, including hip-baths, shower baths and plunge baths. 36 pages and available from the American Antiquarian Society, Worcester, Mass.

DENNING, E.J. & Co., New York, N.Y.; c. 1890 catalog of furnishings for homes, hotels, railroads, institutions. Includes baby carriages, refrigerators, furniture, woodenware sundries. 48 pages. Available from the "Spinning Wheel" magazine library, Hanover, Penn.

Public collections of commercial woodenware and other wood objects

The following public historical and art museums have indicated that they do have within their holdings more than a few pieces of woodenware, wooden sundries for the kitchen, children's carriages, wood refrigerators or children's wooden toys of American manufacture in the second half of the nineteenth century. Some of these museums, as well as others not on this list, have substantial collections of earlier, hand-crafted wood kitchenware, toys and tools.

In some cases, the museum visitor will find items such as Mace produced on permanent display; other pieces may be hidden in storage.

Brooklyn Museum, Brooklyn, N.Y.
Chicago Historical Society, Chicago, Ill.
Children's Museum of Indianapolis, Indianapolis, Ind.
Cincinnati Art Museum, Cincinnati, Ohio
Collection of American Art, Arizona State University, Tempe, Ariz.
Dallas Museum of Fine Arts, Dallas, Texas
Fine Arts Gallery of San Diego, San Diego, Calif.
Florida State Museum, Gainesville, Fla.
Henry Ford Museum & Greenfield Village, Dearborn, Mich.
Indiana University Museum, Bloomington, Ind.
Metropolitan Museum, New York, N.Y.
Michigan Historical Commission Museum, Lansing, Mich.
Minnesota Historical Society Museum, St. Paul, Minn.
Missouri Historical Society, St. Louis, Mo.
Museum of the City of New York, New York, N.Y.
Museum of History and Industry, Seattle, Wash.
New Jersey Historical Society, Newark, N.J.
New York Historical Society, New York, N.Y.
New York State Historical Association, Cooperstown, N.Y.
Ohio Historical Society, Columbus, Ohio
Shelburne Museum, Shelburne, Vt.
Smithsonian Institution, Fine Arts Museum, Washington, D.C.
Smithsonian Institution, Museum of History and Technology, Washington, D.C.
South Dakota State Historical Society, Pierre, S.D.

State Capitol Historical Museum, Olympia, Wash.
State Historical Society of Wisconsin, Madison, Wis.
Staten Island Historical Society, Richmond, S.I., N.Y.
William Penn Memorial Museum, Harrisburg, Penn.
Witte Memorial Museum, San Antonio, Texas